FRUIT OF
THE SPIRIT

FOOD DIARY

ONE

R Mareshah

P.O. Box 4151

Long Branch, NJ 07740

ISBN 978-1-73236-540-7

Month One

God is LOVE! He created you with a loving purpose behind your strengths, weaknesses, physical appearance, experiences, and life span development. Life manifests in wonderful ways when LOVE enhances in your daily walk. Life has its difficulties. This amplifies when a person feels unloved, unlovable, and hateful. You are loved, loveable, and loving. Nourish your body, mind, heart, and spirit with delightful and balanced food choices that are reinforced in your food diary. Food and beverages are necessities for every-day life, health, wellness, and vitality. If there is no LOVE at the core of culinary, domestic, and nutrition practices, the food will not nourish you throughout your body, mind, heart, and spirit. Food nourishes the minds, bodies, hearts, and souls with loving intentions more so than a daily multivitamin ever will. Multivitamins are not effective without having a loving meal beforehand.

Food is not solely a physical process of the digestive system. Every system works in unison to fulfill appropriate function as food travels through the digestive tract. As you nourish yourself, you will be a prominent component on the collective body in your every-day life. Do not punish yourself if a negative thought, feeling, or action manifests before, during, and/or after a food choice. Do not sugarcoat your food choices and feelings associated with them. Healthy living is a marathon and not a sprint. Do not rush your journey. Do not hesitate to write if kale makes you frustrated and cupcakes make you happy. We are human! Write down everything associated with each food choice. Do not hold back. Write down words of profanity if it comes to your mind. Do not worry about what your food diary says. Your diary is a friendly component between you and the Higher Power. A second component of your journey involves self-love. After your last meal, I invite you to write one compliment for yourself. Each day requires space to reflect on a new component of your identity that you love about yourself. You will also write what you love about your food choices each day.

My perspective is your companion with authentic truth, immense sensitivity, no judgment, and no malicious or dishonest intentions that is in the forefront of mainstream sources concerning food and health. Connotative theology influences are unrealistic when human beings are expected to lament every Sunday through Sunday over daily shortcomings and sins. Vulnerable populations feel more guilt and regret more so than those who would soften their hearts and increase spirits of mercy once the truth of a Loving God is reinforced. Reflect on the spirit of LOVE during the first month of your food diary journey. Enjoy the delightful verses and prominent quotes associated with LOVE throughout your first month food diary adventure in the name of LOVE!

Day One: LOVE

Breakfast

Nourishment Choice	Feelings	Thoughts	Actions

Lunch

Nourishment Choice	Feelings	Thoughts	Actions

Snack

Nourishment Choice	Feelings	Thoughts	Actions

Dinner

Nourishment Choice	Feelings	Thoughts	Actions

What I love about myself is

_____

What I love about today's nourishment choices are

_____

Day Two: LOVE

Breakfast

Nourishment Choice	Feelings	Thoughts	Actions

Lunch

Nourishment Choice	Feelings	Thoughts	Actions

Snack

Nourishment Choice	Feelings	Thoughts	Actions

Dinner

Nourishment Choice	Feelings	Thoughts	Actions

What I love about myself is

_____

What I love about today's nourishment choices are

_____

Day Three: LOVE

Breakfast

Nourishment Choice	Feelings	Thoughts	Actions

Lunch

Nourishment Choice	Feelings	Thoughts	Actions

Snack

Nourishment Choice	Feelings	Thoughts	Actions

Dinner

Nourishment Choice	Feelings	Thoughts	Actions

What I love about myself is

_____

What I love about today's nourishment choices are

_____

KEEP LOVE IN YOUR HEART. A LIFE WITHOUT IT IS LIKE A SUNLESS GARDEN WHEN THE FLOWERS ARE DEAD. THE CONSCIOUSNESS OF LOVING AND BEING LOVED BRINGS A WARMTH AND A RICHNESS TO LIFE THAT NOTHING ELSE CAN BRING.

Oscar Wilde

Day Four: LOVE

Breakfast

Nourishment Choice	Feelings	Thoughts	Actions

Lunch

Nourishment Choice	Feelings	Thoughts	Actions

Snack

Nourishment Choice	Feelings	Thoughts	Actions

Dinner

Nourishment Choice	Feelings	Thoughts	Actions

What I love about myself is

_____

What I love about today's nourishment choices are

_____

Day Five: LOVE

Breakfast

Nourishment Choice	Feelings	Thoughts	Actions

Lunch

Nourishment Choice	Feelings	Thoughts	Actions

Snack

Nourishment Choice	Feelings	Thoughts	Actions

Dinner

Nourishment Choice	Feelings	Thoughts	Actions

What I love about myself is

_____

What I love about today's nourishment choices are

_____

Day Six: LOVE

Breakfast

Nourishment Choice	Feelings	Thoughts	Actions

Lunch

Nourishment Choice	Feelings	Thoughts	Actions

Snack

Nourishment Choice	Feelings	Thoughts	Actions

Dinner

Nourishment Choice	Feelings	Thoughts	Actions

What I love about myself is

_____

What I love about today's nourishment choices are

_____

"To love oneself
is the beginning of a lifelong romance."
- Oscar Wilde

self
esteem

Day Seven: LOVE

Breakfast

Nourishment Choice	Feelings	Thoughts	Actions

Lunch

Nourishment Choice	Feelings	Thoughts	Actions

Snack

Nourishment Choice	Feelings	Thoughts	Actions

Dinner

Nourishment Choice	Feelings	Thoughts	Actions

What I love about myself is

_____

What I love about today's nourishment choices are

_____

Day Eight: LOVE

Breakfast

Nourishment Choice	Feelings	Thoughts	Actions

Lunch

Nourishment Choice	Feelings	Thoughts	Actions

Snack

Nourishment Choice	Feelings	Thoughts	Actions

Dinner

Nourishment Choice	Feelings	Thoughts	Actions

What I love about myself is

_____

What I love about today's nourishment choices are

_____

Day Nine: LOVE

Breakfast

Nourishment Choice	Feelings	Thoughts	Actions

Lunch

Nourishment Choice	Feelings	Thoughts	Actions

Snack

Nourishment Choice	Feelings	Thoughts	Actions

Dinner

Nourishment Choice	Feelings	Thoughts	Actions

What I love about myself is

_____

What I love about today's nourishment choices are

_____

♥♥<u>Self Love</u>♥♥

Is

The

Cure

To

~~Self Hate~~

Tyrese Gibson

Day Ten: LOVE

Breakfast

Nourishment Choice	Feelings	Thoughts	Actions

Lunch

Nourishment Choice	Feelings	Thoughts	Actions

Snack

Nourishment Choice	Feelings	Thoughts	Actions

Dinner

Nourishment Choice	Feelings	Thoughts	Actions

What I love about myself is

_____

What I love about today's nourishment choices are

_____

Day Eleven: LOVE

Breakfast

Nourishment Choice	Feelings	Thoughts	Actions

Lunch

Nourishment Choice	Feelings	Thoughts	Actions

Snack

Nourishment Choice	Feelings	Thoughts	Actions

Dinner

Nourishment Choice	Feelings	Thoughts	Actions

What I love about myself is

_____

What I love about today's nourishment choices are

_____

Day Twelve: LOVE

Breakfast

Nourishment Choice	Feelings	Thoughts	Actions

Lunch

Nourishment Choice	Feelings	Thoughts	Actions

Snack

Nourishment Choice	Feelings	Thoughts	Actions

Dinner

Nourishment Choice	Feelings	Thoughts	Actions

What I love about myself is

_____

What I love about today's nourishment choices are

_____

LOVE
is a fruit in season
at all times, anc within
the reach of every hand.

Mother Teresa

Day Thirteen: LOVE

Breakfast

Nourishment Choice	Feelings	Thoughts	Actions

Lunch

Nourishment Choice	Feelings	Thoughts	Actions

Snack

Nourishment Choice	Feelings	Thoughts	Actions

Dinner

Nourishment Choice	Feelings	Thoughts	Actions

What I love about myself is

_____

What I love about today's nourishment choices are

_____

Day Fourteen: LOVE

Breakfast

Nourishment Choice	Feelings	Thoughts	Actions

Lunch

Nourishment Choice	Feelings	Thoughts	Actions

Snack

Nourishment Choice	Feelings	Thoughts	Actions

Dinner

Nourishment Choice	Feelings	Thoughts	Actions

What I love abcut myself is

_____

What I love about today's nourishment choices are

_____

Day Fifteen: LOVE

Breakfast

Nourishment Choice	Feelings	Thoughts	Actions

Lunch

Nourishment Choice	Feelings	Thoughts	Actions

Snack

Nourishment Choice	Feelings	Thoughts	Actions

Dinner

Nourishment Choice	Feelings	Thoughts	Actions

What I love about myself is

_____

What I love about today's nourishment choices are

_____

Life is the Flower
Love is the Honey

Day Sixteen: LOVE

Breakfast

Nourishment Choice	Feelings	Thoughts	Actions

Lunch

Nourishment Choice	Feelings	Thoughts	Actions

Snack

Nourishment Choice	Feelings	Thoughts	Actions

Dinner

Nourishment Choice	Feelings	Thoughts	Actions

What I love about myself is

_____

What I love about today's nourishment choices are

_____

Day Seventeen: LOVE

Breakfast

Nourishment Choice	Feelings	Thoughts	Actions

Lunch

Nourishment Choice	Feelings	Thoughts	Actions

Snack

Nourishment Choice	Feelings	Thoughts	Actions

Dinner

Nourishment Choice	Feelings	Thoughts	Actions

What I love about myself is

_____

What I love about today's nourishment choices are

_____

Day Eighteen: LOVE

Breakfast

Nourishment Choice	Feelings	Thoughts	Actions

Lunch

Nourishment Choice	Feelings	Thoughts	Actions

Snack

Nourishment Choice	Feelings	Thoughts	Actions

Dinner

Nourishment Choice	Feelings	Thoughts	Actions

What I love about myself is

_____

What I love about today's nourishment choices are

_____

Let all
that you do
be done in
Love.

1 Corinthians 16:14

Day Nineteen: LOVE

Breakfast

Nourishment Choice	Feelings	Thoughts	Actions

Lunch

Nourishment Choice	Feelings	Thoughts	Actions

Snack

Nourishment Choice	Feelings	Thoughts	Actions

Dinner

Nourishment Choice	Feelings	Thoughts	Actions

What I love about myself is

_____

What I love about today's nourishment choices are

_____

Day Twenty: LOVE

Breakfast

Nourishment Choice	Feelings	Thoughts	Actions

Lunch

Nourishment Choice	Feelings	Thoughts	Actions

Snack

Nourishment Choice	Feelings	Thoughts	Actions

Dinner

Nourishment Choice	Feelings	Thoughts	Actions

What I love about myself is

_____

What I love about today's nourishment choices are

_____

Day Twenty-One: LOVE

Breakfast

Nourishment Choice	Feelings	Thoughts	Actions

Lunch

Nourishment Choice	Feelings	Thoughts	Actions

Snack

Nourishment Choice	Feelings	Thoughts	Actions

Dinner

Nourishment Choice	Feelings	Thoughts	Actions

What I love about myself is

_____

What I love about today's nourishment choices are

_____

For God
So loved the world
that He gave His
only
Begotten
Son
that whosoever
belIeveth
in Him shall
have everlasting
life.

John 3:16 ♥

Day Twenty-Two: LOVE

Breakfast

Nourishment Choice	Feelings	Thoughts	Actions

Lunch

Nourishment Choice	Feelings	Thoughts	Actions

Snack

Nourishment Choice	Feelings	Thoughts	Actions

Dinner

Nourishment Choice	Feelings	Thoughts	Actions

What I love about myself is

_____

What I love about today's nourishment choices are

_____

Day Twenty-Three: LOVE

Breakfast

Nourishment Choice	Feelings	Thoughts	Actions

Lunch

Nourishment Choice	Feelings	Thoughts	Actions

Snack

Nourishment Choice	Feelings	Thoughts	Actions

Dinner

Nourishment Choice	Feelings	Thoughts	Actions

What I love about myself is

_____

What I love about today's nourishment choices are

_____

Day Twenty-Four: LOVE

Breakfast

Nourishment Choice	Feelings	Thoughts	Actions

Lunch

Nourishment Choice	Feelings	Thoughts	Actions

Snack

Nourishment Choice	Feelings	Thoughts	Actions

Dinner

Nourishment Choice	Feelings	Thoughts	Actions

What I love about myself is

_____

What I love about today's nourishment choices are

_____

choose your
LOVE
love your
CHOICE

Day Twenty-Five: LOVE

Breakfast

Nourishment Choice	Feelings	Thoughts	Actions

Lunch

Nourishment Choice	Feelings	Thoughts	Actions

Snack

Nourishment Choice	Feelings	Thoughts	Actions

Dinner

Nourishment Choice	Feelings	Thoughts	Actions

What I love about myself is

_____

What I love about today's nourishment choices are

_____

Day Twenty-Six: LOVE

Breakfast

Nourishment Choice	Feelings	Thoughts	Actions

Lunch

Nourishment Choice	Feelings	Thoughts	Actions

Snack

Nourishment Choice	Feelings	Thoughts	Actions

Dinner

Nourishment Choice	Feelings	Thoughts	Actions

What I love about myself is

_____

What I love about today's nourishment choices are

_____

Day Twenty-Seven: LOVE

Breakfast

Nourishment Choice	Feelings	Thoughts	Actions

Lunch

Nourishment Choice	Feelings	Thoughts	Actions

Snack

Nourishment Choice	Feelings	Thoughts	Actions

Dinner

Nourishment Choice	Feelings	Thoughts	Actions

What I love about myself is

_____

What I love about today's nourishment choices are

_____

YOU ARE LOVED

Day Twenty-Eight: LOVE

Breakfast

Nourishment Choice	Feelings	Thoughts	Actions

Lunch

Nourishment Choice	Feelings	Thoughts	Actions

Snack

Nourishment Choice	Feelings	Thoughts	Actions

Dinner

Nourishment Choice	Feelings	Thoughts	Actions

What I love about myself is

_____

What I love about today's nourishment choices are

_____

Day Nine: LOVE

Day Twenty-Nine: LOVE

Breakfast

Nourishment Choice	Feelings	Thoughts	Actions

Lunch

Nourishment Choice	Feelings	Thoughts	Actions

Snack

Nourishment Choice	Feelings	Thoughts	Actions

Dinner

Nourishment Choice	Feelings	Thoughts	Actions

What I love about myself is

_____

What I love about today's nourishment choices are

_____

Day Thirty: LOVE

Breakfast

Nourishment Choice	Feelings	Thoughts	Actions

Lunch

Nourishment Choice	Feelings	Thoughts	Actions

Snack

Nourishment Choice	Feelings	Thoughts	Actions

Dinner

Nourishment Choice	Feelings	Thoughts	Actions

What I love about myself is

_____

What I love about today's nourishment choices are

♥ ♥Love the Life ♥ ♥

you

Live

♥ ♥Live the Life ♥ ♥

you

Love

Bob Marley

MONTH TWO

"A joyful heart is good medicine, but a crushed spirit dries up the bones." Proverbs 17:22

How does it feel after devoting a full month to enhancing love within your heart? The first emotion must be pure happiness- JOY! JOY is the next fruit of the spirit that we are going to cultivate. Love is an action word. Joy is a benevolent byproduct and concept that grows from a loving heart. JOY is a noun. Nouns are either people, places, things, and ideas. Think about what people you are around while eating. Think about the locations that you eat in. Think about the things you eat. Think about the things around you while eating. Think about concepts and ideas that surround your inner and outer being while consuming food. Is JOY reflected in every noun in your life? We will meditate on your JOY. We will restore and multiply your JOY this month.

Actions and behaviors stem from feelings. Look back at your food diary charts from the previous month. How many times did you mention "happy" as a listed feeling? Was "happy" ever listed at all? Was the counter emotion of sadness listed? I invite you to analyze your pattern of feelings. Do you feel more JOY during a certain meal? Do you feel sad during a certain meal? Do you have more JOY during breakfast, lunch, snack, or dinner? Are you sad during breakfast, lunch, snack, or dinner? Are you filled with JOY in the morning, afternoon, or evening? Does sadness take over in the morning, afternoon, or evening? Does "junk food" increase or decrease your JOY? Are you JOYFUL after eating "healthy food"? Does "healthy food" or "junk food" increase sadness? Are you happier while eating from a certain food group? Do fruits, vegetables, grains, dairy, or protein choices make you more JOYFUL? Do any specific classifications of food increase your sadness? Are you JOYFUL when eating alone or among a group? Are you sad when eating alone or socially? Is JOY present while eating alone or socially? These are questions that will be answered during your expedition of JOY.

The connection to JOY and food is sacred and intimate. However, there are those who view eating as a fearful and sad ritual. There is fear of weight gain among individuals with anorexia nervosa and bulimia nervosa. There is fear of eating in front of others among those with social anxiety. There are environments that should be safe but recollect trauma when visited again. This month is devoted to restoring the JOY of food and health. Each day, you are delightfully invited to write one element of your life that brings you JOY. You are also invited to write how your food and beverage choices brought you JOY each day. Do not hesitate to write if chocolate brings you joy as opposed to a salad. This journey is about the fruits within your spirit. This journal is nourishing your mind, body, heart, and spirit through the written word.

Day One: JOY

Breakfast

Nourishment Choice	Feelings	Thoughts	Actions

Lunch

Nourishment Choice	Feelings	Thoughts	Actions

Snack

Nourishment Choice	Feelings	Thoughts	Actions

Dinner

Nourishment Choice	Feelings	Thoughts	Actions

I feel joy when…

_____

Today's nourishment choices bring me joy because…

_____

Day Two: JOY

Breakfast

Nourishment Choice	Feelings	Thoughts	Actions

Lunch

Nourishment Choice	Feelings	Thoughts	Actions

Snack

Nourishment Choice	Feelings	Thoughts	Actions

Dinner

Nourishment Choice	Feelings	Thoughts	Actions

I feel joy when…

_____

Today's nourishment choices bring me joy because…

_____

Day Three: JOY

Breakfast

Nourishment Choice	Feelings	Thoughts	Actions

Lunch

Nourishment Choice	Feelings	Thoughts	Actions

Snack

Nourishment Choice	Feelings	Thoughts	Actions

Dinner

Nourishment Choice	Feelings	Thoughts	Actions

I feel joy when…

_____

Today's nourishment choices bring me joy because…

_____

is prayer;
is strength;
is love;
is a net of
love by which
you can catch
souls.

-Mother Teresa

#ChooseJoy

Day Four: JOY

Breakfast

Nourishment Choice	Feelings	Thoughts	Actions

Lunch

Nourishment Choice	Feelings	Thoughts	Actions

Snack

Nourishment Choice	Feelings	Thoughts	Actions

Dinner

Nourishment Choice	Feelings	Thoughts	Actions

I feel joy when…

_____

Today's nourishment choices bring me joy because…

_____

Day Five: JOY

Breakfast

Nourishment Choice	Feelings	Thoughts	Actions

Lunch

Nourishment Choice	Feelings	Thoughts	Actions

Snack

Nourishment Choice	Feelings	Thoughts	Actions

Dinner

Nourishment Choice	Feelings	Thoughts	Actions

I feel joy when…

_____

Today's nourishment choices bring me joy because…

_____

Day Six: JOY

Breakfast

Nourishment Choice	Feelings	Thoughts	Actions

Lunch

Nourishment Choice	Feelings	Thoughts	Actions

Snack

Nourishment Choice	Feelings	Thoughts	Actions

Dinner

Nourishment Choice	Feelings	Thoughts	Actions

I feel joy when…

_____

Today's nourishment choices bring me joy because…

_____

Day Seven: JOY

Breakfast

Nourishment Choice	Feelings	Thoughts	Actions

Lunch

Nourishment Choice	Feelings	Thoughts	Actions

Snack

Nourishment Choice	Feelings	Thoughts	Actions

Dinner

Nourishment Choice	Feelings	Thoughts	Actions

I feel joy when…

_____

Today's nourishment choices bring me joy because…

_____

Day Eight: JOY

Breakfast

Nourishment Choice	Feelings	Thoughts	Actions

Lunch

Nourishment Choice	Feelings	Thoughts	Actions

Snack

Nourishment Choice	Feelings	Thoughts	Actions

Dinner

Nourishment Choice	Feelings	Thoughts	Actions

I feel joy when…

_____

Today's nourishment choices bring me joy because…

_____

Day Nine: JOY

Breakfast

Nourishment Choice	Feelings	Thoughts	Actions

Lunch

Nourishment Choice	Feelings	Thoughts	Actions

Snack

Nourishment Choice	Feelings	Thoughts	Actions

Dinner

Nourishment Choice	Feelings	Thoughts	Actions

I feel joy when…

_____

Today's nourishment choices bring me joy because…

_____

66 The root of joy
is gratefulness. **99**

-David Steindl-Rast

Day Ten: JOY

Breakfast

Nourishment Choice	Feelings	Thoughts	Actions

Lunch

Nourishment Choice	Feelings	Thoughts	Actions

Snack

Nourishment Choice	Feelings	Thoughts	Actions

Dinner

Nourishment Choice	Feelings	Thoughts	Actions

I feel joy when…

_____

Today's nourishment choices bring me joy because…

_____

Day Eleven: JOY

Breakfast

Nourishment Choice	Feelings	Thoughts	Actions

Lunch

Nourishment Choice	Feelings	Thoughts	Actions

Snack

Nourishment Choice	Feelings	Thoughts	Actions

Dinner

Nourishment Choice	Feelings	Thoughts	Actions

I feel joy when…

_____

Today's nourishment choices bring me joy because…

_____

Day Twelve: JOY

Breakfast

Nourishment Choice	Feelings	Thoughts	Actions

Lunch

Nourishment Choice	Feelings	Thoughts	Actions

Snack

Nourishment Choice	Feelings	Thoughts	Actions

Dinner

Nourishment Choice	Feelings	Thoughts	Actions

I feel joy when…

_____

Today's nourishment choices bring me joy because…

_____

Worry
doesn't prevent
disaster
it prevents
Joy!

Day Thirteen: JOY

Breakfast

Nourishment Choice	Feelings	Thoughts	Actions

Lunch

Nourishment Choice	Feelings	Thoughts	Actions

Snack

Nourishment Choice	Feelings	Thoughts	Actions

Dinner

Nourishment Choice	Feelings	Thoughts	Actions

I feel joy when…

_____

Today's nourishment choices bring me joy because…

_____

Day Fourteen: JOY

Breakfast

Nourishment Choice	Feelings	Thoughts	Actions

Lunch

Nourishment Choice	Feelings	Thoughts	Actions

Snack

Nourishment Choice	Feelings	Thoughts	Actions

Dinner

Nourishment Choice	Feelings	Thoughts	Actions

I feel joy when…

_____

Today's nourishment choices bring me joy because…

_____

Day Fifteen: JOY

Breakfast

Nourishment Choice	Feelings	Thoughts	Actions

Lunch

Nourishment Choice	Feelings	Thoughts	Actions

Snack

Nourishment Choice	Feelings	Thoughts	Actions

Dinner

Nourishment Choice	Feelings	Thoughts	Actions

I feel joy when…

_____

Today's nourishment choices bring me joy because…

_____

"If you carry

😊JOY😊

in your

♥**HEART**♥

you can

HEAL

at

ANY MOMENT"

♬ ♪ ♩Carlos Santana♩ ♪ ♬

Day Sixteen: JOY

Breakfast

Nourishment Choice	Feelings	Thoughts	Actions

Lunch

Nourishment Choice	Feelings	Thoughts	Actions

Snack

Nourishment Choice	Feelings	Thoughts	Actions

Dinner

Nourishment Choice	Feelings	Thoughts	Actions

I feel joy when…

_____

Today's nourishment choices bring me joy because…

_____

Day Seventeen: JOY

Breakfast

Nourishment Choice	Feelings	Thoughts	Actions

Lunch

Nourishment Choice	Feelings	Thoughts	Actions

Snack

Nourishment Choice	Feelings	Thoughts	Actions

Dinner

Nourishment Choice	Feelings	Thoughts	Actions

I feel joy when...

_____

Today's nourishment choices bring me joy because...

_____

Day Eighteen: JOY

Breakfast

Nourishment Choice	Feelings	Thoughts	Actions

Lunch

Nourishment Choice	Feelings	Thoughts	Actions

Snack

Nourishment Choice	Feelings	Thoughts	Actions

Dinner

Nourishment Choice	Feelings	Thoughts	Actions

I feel joy when…

_____

Today's nourishment choices bring me joy because…

_____

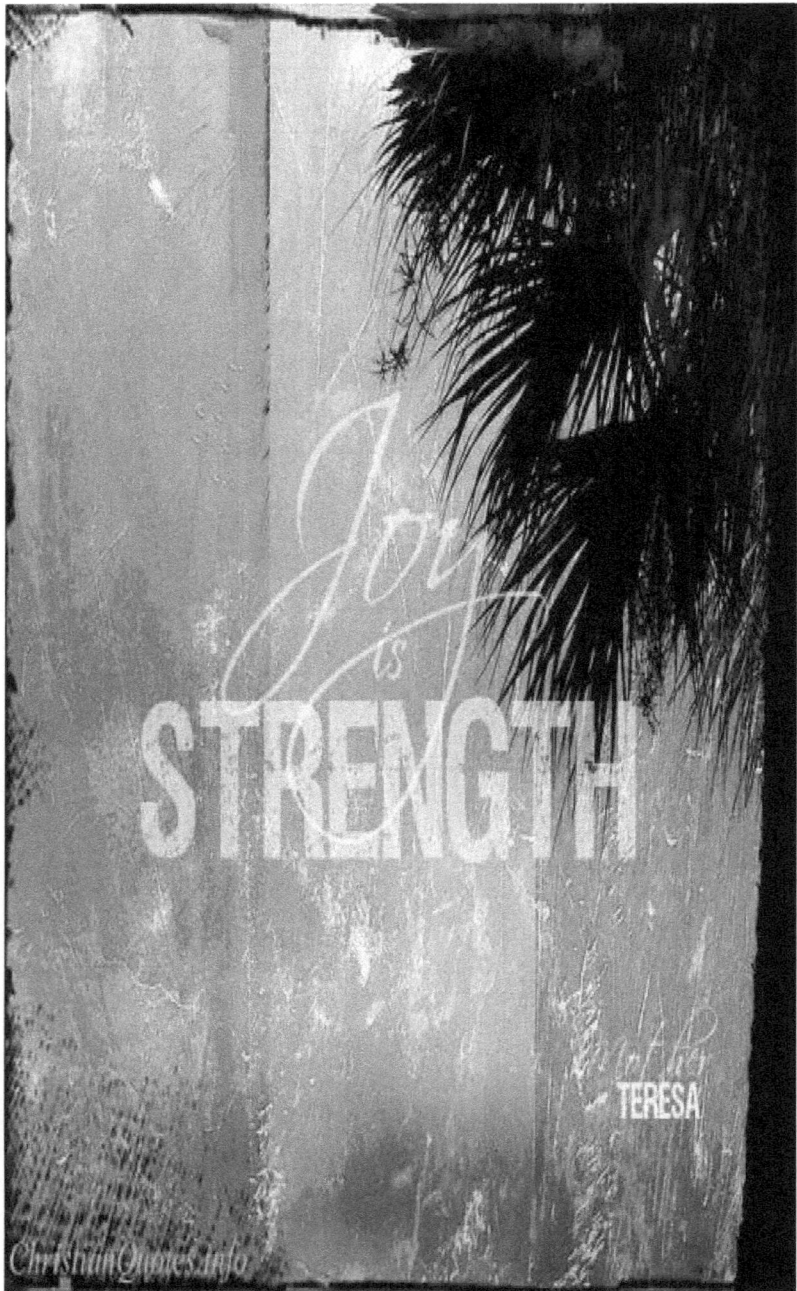

Joy is STRENGTH

TERESA

Day Nineteen: JOY

Breakfast

Nourishment Choice	Feelings	Thoughts	Actions

Lunch

Nourishment Choice	Feelings	Thoughts	Actions

Snack

Nourishment Choice	Feelings	Thoughts	Actions

Dinner

Nourishment Choice	Feelings	Thoughts	Actions

I feel joy when...

_____

Today's nourishment choices bring me joy because...

_____

Day Twenty: JOY

Breakfast

Nourishment Choice	Feelings	Thoughts	Actions

Lunch

Nourishment Choice	Feelings	Thoughts	Actions

Snack

Nourishment Choice	Feelings	Thoughts	Actions

Dinner

Nourishment Choice	Feelings	Thoughts	Actions

I feel joy when…

_____

Today's nourishment choices bring me joy because…

_____

Day Twenty-One: JOY

Breakfast

Nourishment Choice	Feelings	Thoughts	Actions

Lunch

Nourishment Choice	Feelings	Thoughts	Actions

Snack

Nourishment Choice	Feelings	Thoughts	Actions

Dinner

Nourishment Choice	Feelings	Thoughts	Actions

I feel joy when…

_____

Today's nourishment choices bring me joy because…

_____

The

noblest

pleasure

is the

☺ **JOY** ☺

of UNDERSTANDING

Leonardo da Vinci

Day Twenty-Two: JOY

Breakfast

Nourishment Choice	Feelings	Thoughts	Actions

Lunch

Nourishment Choice	Feelings	Thoughts	Actions

Snack

Nourishment Choice	Feelings	Thoughts	Actions

Dinner

Nourishment Choice	Feelings	Thoughts	Actions

I feel joy when…

_____

Today's nourishment choices bring me joy because…

_____

Day Twenty-Three: JOY

Breakfast

Nourishment Choice	Feelings	Thoughts	Actions

Lunch

Nourishment Choice	Feelings	Thoughts	Actions

Snack

Nourishment Choice	Feelings	Thoughts	Actions

Dinner

Nourishment Choice	Feelings	Thoughts	Actions

I feel joy when…

_____

Today's nourishment choices bring me joy because…

_____

Day Twenty-Four: JOY

Breakfast

Nourishment Choice	Feelings	Thoughts	Actions

Lunch

Nourishment Choice	Feelings	Thoughts	Actions

Snack

Nourishment Choice	Feelings	Thoughts	Actions

Dinner

Nourishment Choice	Feelings	Thoughts	Actions

I feel joy when…

_____

Today's nourishment choices bring me joy because…

_____

YOU WILL FIND A *joy*
IN OVERCOMING OBSTACLES

-Helen Keller

Day Twenty-Five: JOY

Breakfast

Nourishment Choice	Feelings	Thoughts	Actions

Lunch

Nourishment Choice	Feelings	Thoughts	Actions

Snack

Nourishment Choice	Feelings	Thoughts	Actions

Dinner

Nourishment Choice	Feelings	Thoughts	Actions

I feel joy when…

_____

Today's nourishment choices bring me joy because…

_____

Day Twenty-Six: JOY

Breakfast

Nourishment Choice	Feelings	Thoughts	Actions

Lunch

Nourishment Choice	Feelings	Thoughts	Actions

Snack

Nourishment Choice	Feelings	Thoughts	Actions

Dinner

Nourishment Choice	Feelings	Thoughts	Actions

I feel joy when…

_____

Today's nourishment choices bring me joy because…

_____

Day Twenty-Seven: JOY

Breakfast

Nourishment Choice	Feelings	Thoughts	Actions

Lunch

Nourishment Choice	Feelings	Thoughts	Actions

Snack

Nourishment Choice	Feelings	Thoughts	Actions

Dinner

Nourishment Choice	Feelings	Thoughts	Actions

I feel joy when…

_____

Today's nourishment choices bring me joy because…

_____

Day Twenty-Eight: JOY

Breakfast

Nourishment Choice	Feelings	Thoughts	Actions

Lunch

Nourishment Choice	Feelings	Thoughts	Actions

Snack

Nourishment Choice	Feelings	Thoughts	Actions

Dinner

Nourishment Choice	Feelings	Thoughts	Actions

I feel joy when…

_____

Today's nourishment choices bring me joy because…

_____

Day Twenty-Nine: JOY

Breakfast

Nourishment Choice	Feelings	Thoughts	Actions

Lunch

Nourishment Choice	Feelings	Thoughts	Actions

Snack

Nourishment Choice	Feelings	Thoughts	Actions

Dinner

Nourishment Choice	Feelings	Thoughts	Actions

I feel joy when…

_____

Today's nourishment choices bring me joy because…

_____

Day Thirty: JOY

Breakfast

Nourishment Choice	Feelings	Thoughts	Actions

Lunch

Nourishment Choice	Feelings	Thoughts	Actions

Snack

Nourishment Choice	Feelings	Thoughts	Actions

Dinner

Nourishment Choice	Feelings	Thoughts	Actions

I feel joy when…

_____

Today's nourishment choices bring me joy because…

_____

JOY is not
in things,
it is...in us.

MONTH THREE

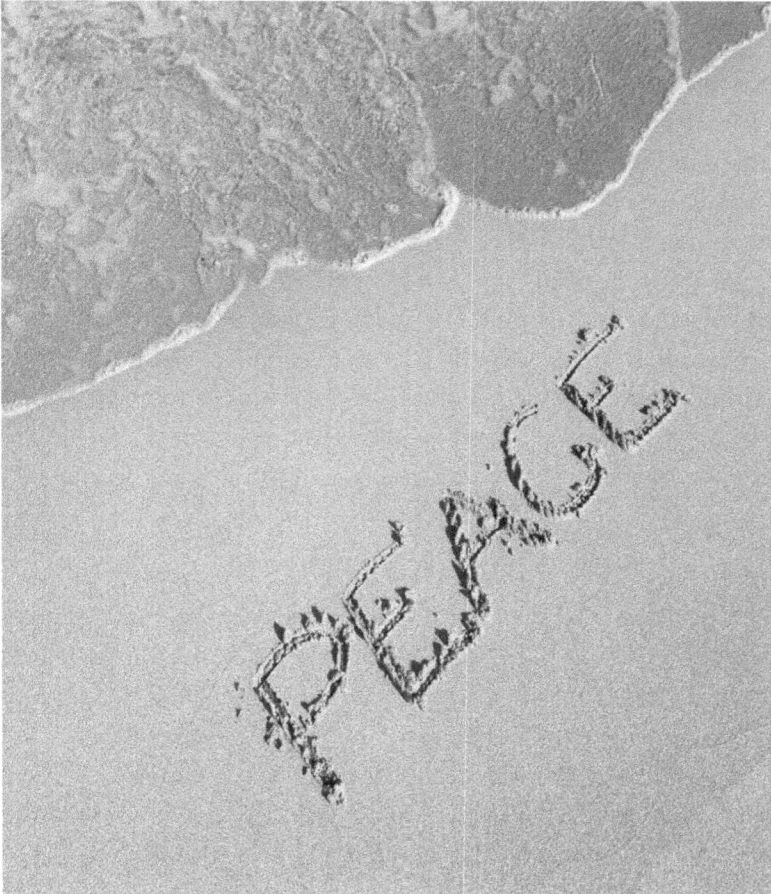

♩♪♫♫ "All we are saying is Give
PEACE a Chance!" ♩♪♫♫

Love and Joy must be filled within your Heart these past two months. This energy that rejuvenated throughout the enhancement of Joy is followed by a calming and soothing state of PEACE. The quote in the PEACE introduction is from a song that repeats the quote "All we are saying is give PEACE a chance". Although a simple quote at face value, a profound characteristic of PEACE is reflected. PEACE is received and a decision one must make to have it. Love is an action. Joy is a benevolent state. PEACE is a decision. Decisions manifest from series of feelings and precede actions. Thoughts manifest from the mind and project feelings and actions.

We are going to explore and enhance the spiritual fruit of PEACE. Review the Love and Joy sections of your diary. Was PEACEFUL, tranquil, calm, serene, or any synonymous feeling ever used to describe your emotional state after a meal? Did you feel more PEACEFUL during breakfast, lunch, snack, or dinner? Did you feel more PEACEFUL in the morning or evening? Was PEACE a state after eating certain fruits, vegetables, grains, dairy, or protein sources? Was PEACE obtained after a salty or sugary food choice? The counter emotion is anxiety. Was anxiety present during healthy or unhealthy food choices? Was anxiety increased in the morning, afternoon, or evening? Do certain fruits, vegetables, grains, dairy, or protein source enhance anxiety? Do social food gatherings make you feel PEACE or anxiety? Does isolative eating increase or decrease PEACE? Keep these questions in your mind as you explore your personal connection to what enhances your inner PEACE through nutrition.

I encourage you to reflect every day on the corresponding sections. Reflect on what specifically enhanced your peace in your food choices and life sentiments. Write down one different person, place, thing, idea, or concept each day for thirty days that makes you feel PEACE. I am here for you as you heal and cultivate your sacred and vital spirit and soul!

Day One: PEACE

Breakfast

Nourishment Choice	Feelings	Thoughts	Actions

Lunch

Nourishment Choice	Feelings	Thoughts	Actions

Snack

Nourishment Choice	Feelings	Thoughts	Actions

Dinner

Nourishment Choice	Feelings	Thoughts	Actions

The following [person, place, thing, idea, statement, thought] heightens my peace…

_____

Today's nourishment choices bring me peace because…

_____

Day Two: PEACE

Breakfast

Nourishment Choice	Feelings	Thoughts	Actions

Lunch

Nourishment Choice	Feelings	Thoughts	Actions

Snack

Nourishment Choice	Feelings	Thoughts	Actions

Dinner

Nourishment Choice	Feelings	Thoughts	Actions

The following [person, place, thing, idea, statement, thought] heightens my peace…

_____

Today's nourishment choices bring me peace because…

_____

Day Three: PEACE

Breakfast

Nourishment Choice	Feelings	Thoughts	Actions

Lunch

Nourishment Choice	Feelings	Thoughts	Actions

Snack

Nourishment Choice	Feelings	Thoughts	Actions

Dinner

Nourishment Choice	Feelings	Thoughts	Actions

The following [person, place, thing, idea, statement, thought] heightens my peace…

_____

Today's nourishment choices bring me peace because…

_____

◻☮◻ ✌PEACE✌ ◻☮◻
begins
with
a
☺smile☺
Mother Teresa

Day Four: PEACE

Breakfast

Nourishment Choice	Feelings	Thoughts	Actions

Lunch

Nourishment Choice	Feelings	Thoughts	Actions

Snack

Nourishment Choice	Feelings	Thoughts	Actions

Dinner

Nourishment Choice	Feelings	Thoughts	Actions

The following [person, place, thing, idea, statement, thought] heightens my peace…

_____

Today's nourishment choices bring me peace because…

_____

Day Five: PEACE

Breakfast

Nourishment Choice	Feelings	Thoughts	Actions

Lunch

Nourishment Choice	Feelings	Thoughts	Actions

Snack

Nourishment Choice	Feelings	Thoughts	Actions

Dinner

Nourishment Choice	Feelings	Thoughts	Actions

The following [person, place, thing, idea, statement, thought] heightens my peace…

_____

Today's nourishment choices bring me peace because…

_____

Day Six: PEACE

Breakfast

Nourishment Choice	Feelings	Thoughts	Actions

Lunch

Nourishment Choice	Feelings	Thoughts	Actions

Snack

Nourishment Choice	Feelings	Thoughts	Actions

Dinner

Nourishment Choice	Feelings	Thoughts	Actions

The following [person, place, thing, idea, statement, thought] heightens my peace…

_____

Today's nourishment choices bring me peace because…

_____

You can't buy inner peace
or wisdom with money.
You have to create them

WITHIN YOURSELF.

Dalai Lama

SYMPHONY OF LOVE
Photo by haiyan Leong

Day Seven: PEACE

Breakfast

Nourishment Choice	Feelings	Thoughts	Actions

Lunch

Nourishment Choice	Feelings	Thoughts	Actions

Snack

Nourishment Choice	Feelings	Thoughts	Actions

Dinner

Nourishment Choice	Feelings	Thoughts	Actions

The following [person, place, thing, idea, statement, thought] heightens my peace…

_____

Today's nourishment choices bring me peace because…

_____

Day Eight: PEACE

Breakfast

Nourishment Choice	Feelings	Thoughts	Actions

Lunch

Nourishment Choice	Feelings	Thoughts	Actions

Snack

Nourishment Choice	Feelings	Thoughts	Actions

Dinner

Nourishment Choice	Feelings	Thoughts	Actions

The following [person, place, thing, idea, statement, thought] heightens my peace…

_____

Today's nourishment choices bring me peace because…

_____

Day Nine: PEACE

Breakfast

Nourishment Choice	Feelings	Thoughts	Actions

Lunch

Nourishment Choice	Feelings	Thoughts	Actions

Snack

Nourishment Choice	Feelings	Thoughts	Actions

Dinner

Nourishment Choice	Feelings	Thoughts	Actions

The following [person, place, thing, idea, statement, thought] heightens my peace…

_____

Today's nourishment choices bring me peace because…

_____

You

will never find

☮ ✌PEACE✌ ☮

of

Mind

until you

listen

to your

♥♥Heart♥♥

George Michael

Day Ten: PEACE

Breakfast

Nourishment Choice	Feelings	Thoughts	Actions

Lunch

Nourishment Choice	Feelings	Thoughts	Actions

Snack

Nourishment Choice	Feelings	Thoughts	Actions

Dinner

Nourishment Choice	Feelings	Thoughts	Actions

The following [person, place, thing, idea, statement, thought] heightens my peace…

_____

Today's nourishment choices bring me peace because…

_____

Day Eleven: PEACE

Breakfast

Nourishment Choice	Feelings	Thoughts	Actions

Lunch

Nourishment Choice	Feelings	Thoughts	Actions

Snack

Nourishment Choice	Feelings	Thoughts	Actions

Dinner

Nourishment Choice	Feelings	Thoughts	Actions

The following [person, place, thing, idea, statement, thought] heightens my peace…

_____

Today's nourishment choices bring me peace because…

_____

Day Twelve: PEACE

Breakfast

Nourishment Choice	Feelings	Thoughts	Actions

Lunch

Nourishment Choice	Feelings	Thoughts	Actions

Snack

Nourishment Choice	Feelings	Thoughts	Actions

Dinner

Nourishment Choice	Feelings	Thoughts	Actions

The following [person, place, thing, idea, statement, thought] heightens my peace…

_____

Today's nourishment choices bring me peace because…

_____

A happy heart
is the fruit of
heavenly peace.

Day Thirteen: PEACE

Breakfast

Nourishment Choice	Feelings	Thoughts	Actions

Lunch

Nourishment Choice	Feelings	Thoughts	Actions

Snack

Nourishment Choice	Feelings	Thoughts	Actions

Dinner

Nourishment Choice	Feelings	Thoughts	Actions

The following [person, place, thing, idea, statement, thought] heightens my peace…

_____

Today's nourishment choices bring me peace because…

_____

Day Fourteen: PEACE

Breakfast

Nourishment Choice	Feelings	Thoughts	Actions

Lunch

Nourishment Choice	Feelings	Thoughts	Actions

Snack

Nourishment Choice	Feelings	Thoughts	Actions

Dinner

Nourishment Choice	Feelings	Thoughts	Actions

The following [person, place, thing, idea, statement, thought] heightens my peace…

_____

Today's nourishment choices bring me peace because…

_____

Day Fifteen: PEACE

Breakfast

Nourishment Choice	Feelings	Thoughts	Actions

Lunch

Nourishment Choice	Feelings	Thoughts	Actions

Snack

Nourishment Choice	Feelings	Thoughts	Actions

Dinner

Nourishment Choice	Feelings	Thoughts	Actions

The following [person, place, thing, idea, statement, thought] heightens my peace…

_____

Today's nourishment choices bring me peace because…

_____

Day Sixteen: PEACE

Breakfast

Nourishment Choice	Feelings	Thoughts	Actions

Lunch

Nourishment Choice	Feelings	Thoughts	Actions

Snack

Nourishment Choice	Feelings	Thoughts	Actions

Dinner

Nourishment Choice	Feelings	Thoughts	Actions

The following [person, place, thing, idea, statement, thought] heightens my peace…

_____

Today's nourishment choices bring me peace because…

_____

Day Seventeen: PEACE

Breakfast

Nourishment Choice	Feelings	Thoughts	Actions

Lunch

Nourishment Choice	Feelings	Thoughts	Actions

Snack

Nourishment Choice	Feelings	Thoughts	Actions

Dinner

Nourishment Choice	Feelings	Thoughts	Actions

The following [person, place, thing, idea, statement, thought] heightens my peace…

_____

Today's nourishment choices bring me peace because…

_____

Day Eighteen: PEACE

Breakfast

Nourishment Choice	Feelings	Thoughts	Actions

Lunch

Nourishment Choice	Feelings	Thoughts	Actions

Snack

Nourishment Choice	Feelings	Thoughts	Actions

Dinner

Nourishment Choice	Feelings	Thoughts	Actions

The following [person, place, thing, idea, statement, thought] heightens my peace…

_____

Today's nourishment choices bring me peace because…

_____

☮ ✌**Peace**✌ ☮

Is

It's

Own

Reward

Mahatma Gandhi

Day Nineteen: PEACE

Breakfast

Nourishment Choice	Feelings	Thoughts	Actions

Lunch

Nourishment Choice	Feelings	Thoughts	Actions

Snack

Nourishment Choice	Feelings	Thoughts	Actions

Dinner

Nourishment Choice	Feelings	Thoughts	Actions

The following [person, place, thing, idea, statement, thought] heightens my peace…

_____

Today's nourishment choices bring me peace because…

_____

Day Twenty: PEACE

Breakfast

Nourishment Choice	Feelings	Thoughts	Actions

Lunch

Nourishment Choice	Feelings	Thoughts	Actions

Snack

Nourishment Choice	Feelings	Thoughts	Actions

Dinner

Nourishment Choice	Feelings	Thoughts	Actions

The following [person, place, thing, idea, statement, thought] heightens my peace…

_____

Today's nourishment choices bring me peace because…

_____

Day Twenty-One: PEACE

Breakfast

Nourishment Choice	Feelings	Thoughts	Actions

Lunch

Nourishment Choice	Feelings	Thoughts	Actions

Snack

Nourishment Choice	Feelings	Thoughts	Actions

Dinner

Nourishment Choice	Feelings	Thoughts	Actions

The following [person, place, thing, idea, statement, thought] heightens my peace...

_____

Today's nourishment choices bring me peace because...

_____

Our

☮ ✌PEACE✌ ☮

shall

stand

as

firm

as

rocky

mountains.

William Shakespeare

Day Twenty-Two: PEACE

Breakfast

Nourishment Choice	Feelings	Thoughts	Actions

Lunch

Nourishment Choice	Feelings	Thoughts	Actions

Snack

Nourishment Choice	Feelings	Thoughts	Actions

Dinner

Nourishment Choice	Feelings	Thoughts	Actions

The following [person, place, thing, idea, statement, thought] heightens my peace…

_____

Today's nourishment choices bring me peace because…

_____

Day Twenty-Three: PEACE

Breakfast

Nourishment Choice	Feelings	Thoughts	Actions

Lunch

Nourishment Choice	Feelings	Thoughts	Actions

Snack

Nourishment Choice	Feelings	Thoughts	Actions

Dinner

Nourishment Choice	Feelings	Thoughts	Actions

The following [person, place, thing, idea, statement, thought] heightens my peace…

_____

Today's nourishment choices bring me peace because…

_____

Day Twenty-Four: PEACE

Breakfast

Nourishment Choice	Feelings	Thoughts	Actions

Lunch

Nourishment Choice	Feelings	Thoughts	Actions

Snack

Nourishment Choice	Feelings	Thoughts	Actions

Dinner

Nourishment Choice	Feelings	Thoughts	Actions

The following [person, place, thing, idea, statement, thought] heightens my peace…

_____

Today's nourishment choices bring me peace because…

_____

◻☮ ✌**PEACE**✌ ☮◻

cannot be

kept by

force;

it can

only be

achieved by

understanding.

Albert Einstein

Day Twenty-Five: PEACE

Breakfast

Nourishment Choice	Feelings	Thoughts	Actions

Lunch

Nourishment Choice	Feelings	Thoughts	Actions

Snack

Nourishment Choice	Feelings	Thoughts	Actions

Dinner

Nourishment Choice	Feelings	Thoughts	Actions

The following [person, place, thing, idea, statement, thought] heightens my peace…

_____

Today's nourishment choices bring me peace because…

_____

Day Twenty-Six: PEACE

Breakfast

Nourishment Choice	Feelings	Thoughts	Actions

Lunch

Nourishment Choice	Feelings	Thoughts	Actions

Snack

Nourishment Choice	Feelings	Thoughts	Actions

Dinner

Nourishment Choice	Feelings	Thoughts	Actions

The following [person, place, thing, idea, statement, thought] heightens my peace…

_____

Today's nourishment choices bring me peace because…

_____

Day Twenty-Seven: PEACE

Breakfast

Nourishment Choice	Feelings	Thoughts	Actions

Lunch

Nourishment Choice	Feelings	Thoughts	Actions

Snack

Nourishment Choice	Feelings	Thoughts	Actions

Dinner

Nourishment Choice	Feelings	Thoughts	Actions

The following [person, place, thing, idea, statement, thought] heightens my peace…

_____

Today's nourishment choices bring me peace because…

_____

P E A C E

"When you find peace within yourself, you become the kind of person who can live at peace with others."

— Peace Pilgrim

Day Twenty-Eight: PEACE

Breakfast

Nourishment Choice	Feelings	Thoughts	Actions

Lunch

Nourishment Choice	Feelings	Thoughts	Actions

Snack

Nourishment Choice	Feelings	Thoughts	Actions

Dinner

Nourishment Choice	Feelings	Thoughts	Actions

The following [person, place, thing, idea, statement, thought] heightens my peace...

_____

Today's nourishment choices bring me peace because...

_____

Day Twenty-Nine: PEACE

Breakfast

Nourishment Choice	Feelings	Thoughts	Actions

Lunch

Nourishment Choice	Feelings	Thoughts	Actions

Snack

Nourishment Choice	Feelings	Thoughts	Actions

Dinner

Nourishment Choice	Feelings	Thoughts	Actions

The following [person, place, thing, idea, statement, thought] heightens my peace…

_____

Today's nourishment choices bring me peace because…

_____

Day Thirty: PEACE

Breakfast

Nourishment Choice	Feelings	Thoughts	Actions

Lunch

Nourishment Choice	Feelings	Thoughts	Actions

Snack

Nourishment Choice	Feelings	Thoughts	Actions

Dinner

Nourishment Choice	Feelings	Thoughts	Actions

The following [person, place, thing, idea, statement, thought] heightens my peace…

_____

Today's nourishment choices bring me peace because…

_____

He
That Knows
Patience
Knows
☮ ✌**PEACE**✌ ☮
Chinese Proverb